AMERICAN LANGUAGE
REPRINTS

VOL. 16

EARLY
VOCABULARIES
OF
MOHAWK

by
Harmen Meyndertsz van den Bogaert

and
Nicolaes van Wassenaer and Johannes Megapolensis

STUDIARE · APPLICARE · CREARE

Evolution Publishing
Merchantville, New Jersey

Extracted from:

J. Franklin Jameson, ed. 1909. *Narratives of New Netherland, 1609–1664*. New York: Charles Scribner's Sons.

This edition ©1999 by Evolution Publishing.
an imprint of Arx Publishing, LLC

Originally published in hardcover 1999.
Reprinted in paperback 2023.

Printed in the
United States of America

For Saint Kateri Tekakwitha, the Lily of the Mohawks.

ISSN 1540-3475

ISBN 978-1-935228-29-5

CONTENTS

Preface to the 1999 Edition

A sobering fact of historical research is that important documents are continually lost to the world through neglect or destruction, quite often leaving no trace that they ever existed. It is therefore all the more noteworthy when a long-forgotten source turns up unexpectedly, making accessible new information that would never have been known otherwise.

While in the city of Amsterdam in the summer of 1895, a Scottish-born emigré to America named General James Grant Wilson discovered a 32 page manuscript of a Dutchman's journal of travel through the Mohawk and Oneida country in "New Netherland" (what is now eastern New York State) written in 1634-1635. Realizing its value, Wilson published it immediately (Wilson 1895, 1896), attributing the unsigned manuscript to Arent van Curler, an employee of the Dutch West India Company. Later research (van Laer 1908) showed that van Curler did not arrive at the colony until four years later in 1638, and thus could not have authored the account. Since 1909, when a second edition of the narrative was published (Jameson 1909), scholars have instead attributed its authorship to Harmen Meyndertsz van den Bogaert, the surgeon of Fort Orange (now Albany).

The discovery of van den Bogaert's journal was indeed serendipitous: without it "we would be deprived of the earliest known description of the Lower Iroquois and their environment, including detailed accounts of their settlements, healing rituals, systems of protocol, language, and subsistence practices. It stands as a unique and compelling document." (Bogaert 1988). Particularly useful from the linguist's perspective is a "Vocabulary of the Maquas" appended onto the text of the journal: "Maqua" was the seventeenth century Dutch and English name for the Mohawks, inherited from the Algonquian-speaking Mahicans on the Hudson river among whom the Dutch and English had settled.

The Mohawks were the easternmost tribe of the "Five Nations" Iroquois. Their primary settlements were located along the Mohawk creek in what is now Montgomery County, New York, although they hunted in an area considerably larger, from the Adirondacks to the headwaters of the Susquehanna river.

Sources which deal with the Five Nations Iroquois often use the word "castle" to describe their largest settlements. Like the stone-built European castles of medieval times, an Iroquoian castle was a large (wooden) defensive fortification, as opposed to a "village" which was smaller and undefended. There were apparently three main castles of the seventeenth-century Mohawks: Onekagoncka or Caughnawaga, Kanagaro, and Tionnontoguen (van den Bogaert 1988 note 17, Fenton and Tooker 1978).

Mohawk as a language is well known, having been documented since the mid-1600's. About twenty years ago it was still being spoken by a few thousand people in Quebec, Ontario, and New York State (Mithun 1977). Dialect divisions among modern speakers are slight, as between the Caughnawaga and St. Regis varieties, and thus appear to be of comparatively recent divergence.

2

Other Dutch sources provide bits of linguistic data from New Netherland, some of which will be discussed later, but van den Bogaert's is unusually extensive and quite well done for such an early date, even earning praise from modern-day linguists (Michelson p. 51, in Bogaert 1988). While it is not precisely the first sample of Mohawk ever recorded, it certainly is the first one of any substantial length, totaling about 200 entries for trading goods, animals, social terminology, parts of the body, and other commonly used concepts. Generally, vocabularies at this time were not taken for purely scientific reasons—that day was still far off—but rather for very practical matters such as exploration, trading or treaty negotiations.

From January 1 to January 12, 1635, Van den Bogaert's party made a brief sojourn to Onneyuttehage or Oneida Castle. In the portion of his narrative for these days he gives a number of Iroquoian words which may be Oneida rather than Mohawk.

Van den Bogaert' s account has been published several times since its discovery in the 1890's. We have already mentioned its first two editions by James Grant Wilson (Wilson 1895, 1896) and the 1909 edition of Jameson, from which all of the excerpts in this volume are taken. In the most recent edition (van den Bogaert 1988) the journal was published in a volume by itself. This 1988 edition has copious endnotes with valuable ethno-historical and linguistic notes; in editing the vocabulary Gunther Michelson also includes the original Dutch glosses and provides modern Mohawk words in phonemic notation for comparison.

3

The original manuscript of van den Bogaert's journal, which is currently housed in the Henry E. Huntington Library in San Marino California, was not consulted for this edition, which is based instead on Jameson's published copy. To help alleviate any errors due to inevitable misprints and errors in transcription, I have compared all the Jameson entries with those of the second Wilson edition and the 1988 Gehring-Starna edition, and noted any significant variations (labeled W. and GS. respectively).

Two smaller samples of the Mohawk language were also recorded in the first half of the 17th century. The longer and earlier of the two was written by Nicolaes Janszoon van Wassenaer, a Dutch scholar and physician. Wassenaer's *Historisch Verhael alder ghedenck-weerdichste Geschiedenissen die hier en daer in Europa* or "Historical Account of all the most Remarkable Events which have happened in Europe" was a news digest published in Amsterdam semi-annually from 1621 to 1631. Included therein are various accounts of New Netherland and the Dutch West India company; Wassenaer likely came into contact with settlers and employees of the company who had been in America, and from them he would hear news of the colony.

Under the entry for February 1624 Wassenaer gives the first word-list of Mohawk ever recorded: the numbers from 1-10, and the month names from February—"the first with them"—to November. To these we can add a few more Mohawk words which are scattered around other portions of the text. Wassenaer also gives some other words from the unrelated Algonquian tribes to the east, but these last have not been included in the current edition.

Another seventeenth century word-list of Mohawk is found in "A short account of the Mohawk Indians" (1644) by Johannes Megapolensis. Earlier in his youth, Megapolensis had "relinquished Popery and was thrust out at once from my inherited estate" in other words his rejection of the Catholic faith caused estrangement from his family. His religious inclinations were not squelched but simply redirected, as he subsequently became a devout Protestant and preached in various Holland towns. In 1642 Kiliaen van Rensselaer, the director of the West India Company and patroon of a tract of land on the west bank of the Hudson River, offered Megapolensis a job as the resident clergyman in his domain. Megapolensis accepted, and arrived in New Netherland in August of that same year with his wife and children. Not surprisingly, the Mohawk terms he preserves in his account deal mainly with matters of religion.

Megapolensis' comments on the Mohawk language show a man with keen abilities of comprehension, though understandably constrained by his limited experience. Like most learned Europeans of the time, his grammatical notions were based on Indo-European languages such as Dutch, Latin and Greek; Iroquoian languages were organized along very different principles. Yet he is well aware of the difference between the true Mohawk language and the jargon used by traders—a difference that other Europeans did not so readily detect. Also, he clearly recognizes that his requests for words are being answered in different grammatical constructions.

One gets the feeling that had Megapolensis been able to devote his life's study to the language, he was capable of producing Mohawk materials on par with some of the better linguistic descriptions of the time period. His vocabulary, as far we know, does not survive; nor is it clear whether he even finished it. But the few words he has left add to the earliest recordings of the Mohawk language, and help to extend its documentation back into the dawn of American history.

—Claudio R. Salvucci, series ed.

Bibliography and Recommended Reading

Beatty, John. 1974. *Mohawk Morphology*. Occasional Publications in Anthropology Linguistics Series No. 2. Greeley, Colorado:University of Northern Colorado Museum of Anthropology.

Bogaert, Harmen Meyndertsz van den. 1988. *A journey into Mohawk and Oneida Country, 1634-1635*. Charles T. Gehring and William A. Starna, eds. Syracuse, NY:Syracuse University Press.

Bonvillain, Nancy. 1973. *A Grammar of Akwesasne Mohawk*. National Museum of Man, Ethnology Division, Mercury Series 8. Ottawa.

Fenton, William N. and Elisabeth Tooker. 1978. "Mohawk." in William Sturtevant, Bruce Trigger, eds., *Handbook of North American Indians vol. 15: Northeast*, pp. 446-480. Washington, D.C.:Smithsonian Institution.

Goddard, Ives, ed. 1996. *Handbook of North American Indians vol. 17: Languages*. Washington, D.C.: Smithsonian Institution.

Jameson, J. Franklin, ed. 1909. *Narratives of New Netherland, 1609-1664*. New York:Charles Scribner's Sons.

Lounsbury, Floyd. 1978. "Iroquoian Languages." in William Sturtevant, Bruce Trigger, eds., *Handbook of North American Indians vol. 15: Northeast*, pp. 334-343. Washington, D.C.:Smithsonian Institution.

Mithun, Marianne. 1977. *Iontenwennaweienstahkhwa':
Mohawk Spelling Dictionary.* New York State Museum
and Science Service Bulletin.

Mithun, Marianne. 1979. "Iroquoian" in Lyle Campbell
and Marianne Mithun, eds. *The Languages of Native
America: Historical and Comparative Assessment,* pp.
133-212. Austin:University of Texas Press.

Van Laer, A. J. F. 1908. *Van Rensselaer Bowier Manu-
scripts.* Albany:University of the State of New York.

Wilson, James Grant. 1895. "Corlear and his journal of
1634." *The Independent* 47 (October 3, 1895).

Wilson, James Grant. 1896. "Arent van Curler and His
Journal of 1634-35." *American Historical Association
Annual Report for 1895.* pp. 81-101.

Excerpt from
Narrative of a Journey into the
Mohawk and Oneida Country,
1634-1635

December 13.   In the morning we went together to the
castle over the ice that during the night had frozen on the
kill, and, after going half a league, we arrived in their first
castle, which is built on a high hill. There stood but 36
houses, in rows like streets, so that we could pass nicely.
The houses are made and covered with bark of trees, and
mostly are flat at the top. Some are 100, 90, or 80 paces
long and 22 and 23 feet high. There were some inside
doors of hewn boards, furnished with iron hinges. In some
houses we saw different kinds of iron work, iron chains,
harrow irons, iron hoops, nails—which they steal when
they go forth from here. Most of the people were out
hunting deer and bear. The houses were full of corn that
they call *onersti*, and we saw maize; yes, in some of the
houses more than 300 bushels. They make canoes and
barrels of the bark of trees, and sew with bark as well. We
had a good many pumpkins cooked and baked that they
call *anansira*. None of the chiefs were at home, but the
principal chief is named Adriochten, who lived a quarter
of a mile from the fort in a small house, because a good
many savages here in the castle died of smallpox. I sent
him a message to come and see us, which he did; he came
and bade me welcome, and said that he wanted us very

much to come with him. We should have done so, but when already on the way another chief called us, and so we went to the castle again. This one had a big fire lighted, and a fat haunch of venison cooked, of which we ate. He gave us two bearskins to sleep on, and presented me with three beaver skins. In the evening Willem Tomassen, whose legs were swollen from the march, had a few cuts made with a knife therein, and after that had them rubbed with bear grease. We slept in this house, ate heartily of pumpkins, beans and venison, so that we were not hungry, but were treated as well as is possible in their land. We hope that all will succeed.

—Attributed to Harmen Meyndertsz van den Bogaert, 1634.

MOHAWK— ENGLISH

Achta, *shoes.*

Adenocquat, *to give medicine.*

Aderondackx, *Frenchmen or Englishmen.* W. **aderondacke.**

Adiron, *cat(s).* GS. = "raccoon".

Agetsioga, *a string of beads.* GS. **agotsioha.**

Aghidawe, *to sleep.* W. **aqhidawe.**

Aghihi, *sick.*

Allesa rondade, *fire your pistols.* Also **alle sarondade.** GS. **allese rondade.**

Anansira, *pumpkins.* GS. **anonsira.**

Anesagghena, *Mahicans or Mohigans.*

Anochquis, *hair.*

Anonsi, *head.*

Aquayanderen, *a chief.* W. **aguayanderen.**

Aquayesse, *to laugh.*

Aque (Gario?), *deer.*

Aquesados, *horse.*

Aquidagon, *ox.*

Aquinachoo, *angry.*

Archoo, *at once.*

Asistock, *the stars.*

Assaghe, *rapier.*

Asse, *three.*

Assere, *knives.*

Asserle, *very strong.*

Assire, *cloth.*

Athesera, *flour.*

Atoga, *axes.*
Atsochta, *adze.*
Atsochwat, *tobacco.*
Attochwat, *spoons.*
Augustuske, *in the winter, very cold.*
Awaheya, *death.*
Awahta, *testicles.* GS. **awasta.**

Cadadiene, *to trade.* GS. **cadadiiene.**
Cahonsÿe, *black.*
Cana, *the seed.*
Canadack, *sack or basket.*
Canadaghi, *a castle.*
Canadera, *bread.*
Canaderage, *a river.*
Canagosat, *scraper.* W. **canagoeefat**, GS. **canagoesat.**
Canderes, *phallus.*
Canna warori, *prostitute.*
Canonou, *pipe.*
Cany, *sack or basket.*
Canyewa, *small.*
Carente, *artful, crooked.*
Careyago, *the sky.*
Caris, *stockings.*
Caroo, *close by.*
Casoya, *ship, canoe.*
Cates, *thick.*
Catse (Garistats?), *bell.*

Catteges issewe, *when will you come again?* W. **catteges in sewe**.

Cayanoghe, *islands.*

Cayere, *four.*

Ceheda (Osaheta?), *beans.* W. **echeda**.

Christittye, *iron, copper, or lead.* W. **karistaji**.

Cian, *child.*

Cinsie, *fish.*

Coenhasaren, *to cure.* W. **coengararen**.

Coenhechti (Gahetien?), *a woman.*

Conossade, *house or hut.*

Crage, *white.*

Dadeneye, *to gamble.*

Daweyate, *to sit in council.*

Dedaia witha, *shirts or coats.*

Dequoguoha, *to go hunting.* GS. **dequoquoha**.

Deserentekar, *meadow.* GS = "to graze".

Distan, *mother.*

Eightjen, see **etsi**.

Endatcondere, *to paint.*

Endat hatste, *looking-glass.* GS. **endathatst**.

Esteronde, *the rain.*

Etsi (Eightjen?), *a man.*

Exhechta, *a lass.*

Eyo, *mink.*

Eÿtroghe, *beads.* GS. **eytroghe**.

Gahetien, see **coenhechti**.

Gario, see **aque**.

Garistats, see **catse**.

Garonare, see **kamewari**.

Ghekeront, *salmon.*

Iachte yendere, *'tis no good.*

Ichar, *dog.*

Jaghac teroeni, *frightened.* W. **jaqhae terreni**; GS. **jaghacteroene**.

Jankurangue, *very tired.* GS. **jankanque**.

Jawe Arenias, *thank you Arenias.* [a chief —ed.]

Jayack, *six.*

Joddireyo, *to fight.*

Johati, *a path or road.*

Jorhani, *tomorrow.*

Jori, *it is ready.*

Judicha, *the fire.* W. **judichaga**.

Kahanckt, *geese.*

Kamewari (Garonare?), *awls.* W. **kareenari**, GS. **kamrewari**.

Kanon newage, *Manhattan.*

Karackwero, *the sun.* W. **karaekwero**.

Katkaste, *to cook dinner.*

Katten kerreyager, *very hungry.*

Kayontochke, *flat arable land.*

16

Kewanea, see **quane.**

Keye, *the fat.*

Kragequa, *swans.* W. **uragegua**.

Kristoni asseroni, *Netherlanders, Germans.*

Netho, netho, netho!, *this is very well.* [perhaps Oneida]

Nonnewarory, *fur caps.* W. **nonewarory**.

Ochquari, *bear.*

Ochquoha, *wolf.*

Ocstaha, *an old man.* W., GS. **ochtaha**.

Odasqueta, *an old woman.*

Odossera, *the bacon.*

Oetseira, *fire.*

Oeuda, *excrements.* W. **oerida**.

Oggaha, *cloth.*

Ohochta, *ears.* GS. **ochochta**.

Ohonikwa, *throat.* GS. **ohonckwa**.

Ohonte, *grass, vegetables.*

Onatassa, *fingers.*

Onawÿ, *teeth.*

Onckwe, *men.*

Ondach, *kettles.*

Onea, *stone.*

Onega, *water.*

Oneggeri, *weeds or reeds or straw.*

Onegonsera, *red paint.*

Onekoera, *seawan, their money.*

Onenta, *arm.*

Onentar, *woman in labor.* GS. **oentar**.

Onera, *pudenda.*

Onersti, *corn.* GS. **onesti**.

Oneste, *maize.* W. **oneote**.

Onewachten, *a liar.*

Oneyatsa, *nose.*

Onighira, *to drink.*

Ononda, *mountains.*

Onsaha, *vesicle.*

Onscat, *one.*

Onscat teneyawe, *hundred.*

Onstara, *to weep.*

Onvare, *shoulder blade.* GS. **onirare**.

Oqhoho, *wolf.* GS. **oquoho**.

Orochquine, *spine.* W. **orochguine**.

Osaheta, see **ceheda**.

Oscante, *bark.* GS. **osconte**.

Osnotsa, *hands.*

Osqucha, *I'll fetch it.*

Ossidan, *feet.* W. **ossidari**, GS. **ossidau**.

Ossivenda, *blue.* W. **ossirenda**.

Ostie, *the bone.*

Otich kera, *thumb.*

Otsira, *nails.*

Otteyage, *in the summer.*

Owaetsei, *at present.*

Owanisse, *tongue.*

Oware, *meat.*

Oyendere, *very good.*

Oyente, *wood (firewood).*

Oyere, *ten.*

Oyoghi, *a kill (small river).* GS. **oÿoghi.**

Quane (Kewanea?), *great.*

Rackesie, *cousin.*

Ragenonou, *uncle.* W. **ragenonon.**

Ragina, *father.*

Rocksongwa (Ronwaye?), *boy.*

Rockste, *friends.*

Ronwaye, see **rocksongwa**.

Sagat, *doubly.*

Sari wacksi, *a chatterer.*

Sasaskarisat, *scissors.* GS. **tasaskarisat.**

Sasnoron, *hurry up.* GS. **sastorum.**

Sateeni, *dog.*

Sategat, *to light the fire, make fire.*

Sategon, *eight.* GS. **hategon.**

Satewa, *alone.*

Satsori, *to eat.*

Schascari wanasi, *eagles.*

Schasohadee, *the overside.* W. **nhasohadee**; GS. **schahohadee.**

Schawariwane, *turkeys.*

Senadondo, *fox.*

Senoto wanne, *elk.*

Seranda, *male cat.* GS. = "marten".

Seronquatse, *a scoundrel.*

Seÿendere ü, *I know him well.* GS. **seyendereii**.

Simachkoes, *their doctors.* GS. **sunachkoes**.

Sinachkoo, *to drive the devil away.*

Sine gechtera, *a wooer.*

Sinekaty, *carnal copulation.*

Sinite, *beaver.*

Sintho, *to sow.*

Sorsar, *to raise.*

Tali, *crane.*

Tantanege, *hares.*

Tawasse, *forty.*

Tawÿne, *otter.*

Tegenhondi, *in the spring.* GS. **tegenhonid**.

Tenon commenyon, *what do you want?* W. **tenon connengon**; GS. **tenon commeyon**.

The derri, *yesterday.*

Tiggeni, *two.*

Tiggeretait, *combs.*

Torsas, *to the north.*

Tosenochte, *I don't know.* GS. **tesenochte**.

Tsadack, *seven.*

Tÿochte, *nine.*

Waghideria, *to sweat.*

Welsmachkoo, *you must not lie?* [perhaps Oneida]

Wisch, *five.* GS. **wisck**.

Wistotcera, *the grease.*

Wotstaha, *broad.*

Phrases:

Ha assironi atsimach koo kent oya kayuig wee Onneyatte Onaondaga Koyocke hoo Hanoto wany agweganne hoo schene ha caton scahten franosoni yndicho, that means *I could go in all these places* —they said the names of all the castles—*freely and everywhere. I should be provided with a house and a fire and wood and everything I needed; and if I wanted to go to the Frenchmen they would guide me there and back.* GS. **ha assironi atsimachkoo kent oyakaying wee onneyatte onaondage koyockwe hoo senoto wanyagweganne hoo schenehalaton kasten kanosoni yndicko**.

ENGLISH — MOHAWK

Adze, *atsochta*.
Alone, *satewa*.
Angry, *aquinachoo*.
Arm, *onenta*.
Artful, *carente*.
Awls, *kamewari (garonare?)*.
Axes, *atoga*.

Bacon, the, *odossera*.
Bark, *oscante*.
Basket, *canadack, cany*.
Beads, *eÿtroghe*. **A string of beads**, *agetsioga*.
Beans, *ceheda (osaheta?)*.
Bear, *ochquari*.
Beaver, *sinite*.
Bell, *catse (garistats?)*.
Black, *cahonsÿe*.
Blue, *ossivenda*.
Bone, the, *ostie*.
Boy, *rocksongwa (ronwaye?)*.
Bread, *canadera*.
Broad, *wotstaha*.

Canoe, *casoya*.
Castle, a, *canadaghi*.
Cat, *adiron*.
Cat, male, *seranda*.
Chatterer, a, *sari wacksi*.

Chief, a, *aquayanderen.*
Child, *cian.*
Close by, *caroo.*
Cloth, *assire*, *oggaha.*
Coats, *dedaia witha.*
Cold, very, *augustuske.*
Combs, *tiggeretait.*
Come again, when will you?, *catteges issewe.*
Cook dinner, to, *katkaste.*
Copper, *christittye.*
Copulation, carnal, *sinekaty.*
Corn, *onersti.*
Council, to sit in, *daweyate.*
Cousin, *rackesie.*
Crane, *tali.*
Creek, *oyoghi.*
Crooked, *carente.*
Cure, to, *coenhasaren.*

Death, *awaheya.*
Deer, *aque (gario?).*
Devil, to drive the devil away, *sinachkoo.*
Dinner, to cook, *katkaste.*
Doctors, their, *simachkoes.*
Dog, *ichar* or *sateeni.*
Doubly, *sagat.*
Drink, to, *onighira.*
Drive the devil away, to, *sinachkoo.*

Eagles, *schascari wanasi.*
Ears, *ohochta.*
Eat, to, *satsori.*
Eight, *sategon.*
Elk, *senoto wanne.*
Englishmen, *aderondackx.*
Excrements, *oeuda.*

Fat, the, *keye.*
Father, *ragina.*
Feet, *ossidan.*
Fetch, I'll fetch it, *osqucha.*
Fight, to, *joddireyo.*
Fingers, *onatassa.*
Fire, *oetseira.* **The fire**, *judicha.* **To light the fire**, *sategat.*
   To make fire, *sategat.*
Fire your pistols, *allesa rondade.*
Firewood, *oyente.*
Fish, *cinsie.*
Five, *wisch.*
Flour, *athesera.*
Forty, *tawasse.*
Four, *cayere.*
Fox, *senadondo.*
Frenchmen, *aderondackx.*
Friends, *rockste.*
Frightened, *jaghac teroeni.*
Fur caps, *nonnewarory.*

Gamble, to, *dadeneye.*

Geese, *kahanckt.*

Germans, *kristoni asseroni.*

Give medicine, to, *adenocquat.*

Good, very, *oyendere.* **'Tis no good**, *iachte yendere.*

Grass, *ohonte.*

Grease, the, *wistotcera.*

Great, *quane (kewanea?).*

Hair, *anochquis.*

Hands, *osnotsa.*

Hares, *tantanege.*

Head, *anonsi.*

Horse, *aquesados.*

House, *conossade.*

Hundred, *onscat teneyawe.*

Hungry, very, *katten kerreyager.*

Hunting, to go, *dequoguoha.*

Hurry up, *sasnoron.*

Hut, *conossade.*

Iron, *christittye.*

Islands, *cayanoghe.*

Kettles, *ondach.*

Knives, *assere.*

Know, I don't, *tosenochte.* **I know him well**, *seÿendere ü.*

Land, flat arable, *kayontochke*.
Lass, a, *exhechta*.
Laugh, to, *aquayesse*.
Lead, *christittye*.
Liar, a, *onewachten*.
Light the fire, *sategat*.
Looking-glass, *endat hatste*.

Mahicans, *anesagghena*.
Maize, *oneste*.
Make fire, *sategat*.
Man, a, *etsi (eightjen?)*. **An old man**, *ocstaha*.
Manhattan, *kanon newage*.
Meadow, *deserentekar*.
Meat, *oware*.
Men, *onckwe*.
Mink, *eyo*.
Mohigans, *anesagghena*.
Money, their, *onekoera*.
Mother, *distan*.
Mountains, *ononda*.

Nails, *otsira*.
Netherlanders, *kristoni asseroni*.
Nine, *tÿochte*.
North, to the, *torsas*.
Nose, *oneyatsa*.

Once, at, *archoo*.
One, *onscat*.
Otter, *tawÿne*.
Overside, the, *schasohadee*.
Ox, *aquidagon*.

Paint, to, *endatcondere*. **Red paint**, *onegonsera*.
Path, a, *johati*.
Phallus, *canderes*.
Pipe, *canonou*.
Present, at, *owaetsei*.
Prostitute, *canna warori*.
Pudenda, *onera*.
Pumpkins, *anansira*.

Rain, the, *esteronde*.
Raise, to, *sorsar*.
Rapier, *assaghe*.
Ready, it is, *jori*.
Red paint, *onegonsera*.
Reeds, *oneggeri*.
River, *canaderage*.
Road, *johati*.

Sack, *canadack, cany*.
Salmon, *ghekeront*.
Scissors, *sasaskarisat*.
Scoundrel, a, *seronquatse*.

Scraper, *canagosat.*

Seawan, *onekoera.*

Seed, the, *cana.*

Seven, *tsadack.*

Ship, *casoya.*

Shirts, *dedaia witha.*

Shoes, *achta.*

Shoulder blade, *onvare.*

Sick, *aghihi.*

Sit in council, to, *daweyate.*

Six, *jayack.*

Sky, the, *careyago.*

Sleep to, *aghidawe.*

Small, *canyewa.*

Sow, to, *sintho.*

Spine, *orochquine.*

Spoons, *attochwat.*

Spring, in the, *tegenhondi.*

Stars, the, *asistock.*

Stockings, *caris.*

Stone, *onea.*

Straw, *oneggeri.*

String of beads, a, *agetsioga.*

Strong, very, *asserie.*

Summer, in the, *otteyage.*

Sun, the, *karackwero.*

Swans, *kragequa.*

Sweat, to, *waghideria.*

Teeth, *onawÿ*.
Ten, *oyere*.
Testicles, *awahta*.
Thank you Arenias, *jawe Arenias*.
Thick, *cates*.
Three, *asse*.
Throat, *ohonikwa*.
Thumb, *otich kera*.
Tired, very, *jankurangue*.
Tobacco, *atsochwat*.
Tomorrow, *jorhani*.
Tongue, *owanisse*.
Trade, to, *cadadiene*.
Turkeys, *schawariwane*.
Two, *tiggeni*.

Uncle, *ragenonou*.

Vegetables, *ohonte*.
Vesicle, *onsaha*.

Want, what do you?, *tenon commenyon*.
Water, *onega*.
Weeds, *oneggeri*.
Weep, to, *onstara*.
White, *crage*.
Winter, in the, *augustuske*.
Wolf, *ochquoha, oquoho*.

Woman, a, *coenhechti (gahetien?).* **An old woman**, *odasqueta.* **Woman in labor**, *onentar.*

Wood, *oyente.*

Wooer, a, *sine gechtera.*

Yesterday, *the derri.*

Numerical Table

1. Onscat
2. Tiggeni
3. Asse
4. Cayere
5. Wisch
6. Jayack

7. Tsadack
8. Sategon
9. Tÿochte
10. Oyere
40. Tawasse
100. Onscat teneyawe

MOHAWK NUMERALS
AND MONTH NAMES

Excerpt from Wassenaer's Historical Account

'Tis worthy of remark that, with so many tribes, there is so great a diversity of language. They vary frequently not over five or six leagues; forthwith comes another language; if they meet they can hardly understand one another. There are some who come sixty leagues from the interior, and can not at all understand those on the river...

Their numerals run no higher than ours; twenty being twice ten. When they desire twenty of anything, they stick the ten fingers up and point with them to the feet on which are ten toes. They count, *Honslat, Tegeni, Hasse, Kajeri, Wisk, Iajack, Satach, Siattege, Tiochte, Ojeri.* The names of their months are these: *Cuerano*, the first with them, February; 2 *Weer-hemska*; 3. *Heemskan*; 4. *Oneratacka*; 5. *Oneratack*, then men begin to sow and to plant: 6. *Hagarert*; 7. *Iakouvaratta*; 8. *Hatterhonagat*; 9. *Genhendasta*; then the grain and every thing is ripe. 10. *Digojenjattha*, then is the seed housed. Of January and December they take no note, being of no use to them.

—Nicolaes van Wassenaer, 1624.

Honslat, *one*.
Tegeni, *two*.
Hasse, *three.*
Kajeri, *four*.
Wisk, *five*.
Iajack, *six*.

Satach, *seven.*

Siattege, *eight.*

Tiochte, *nine.*

Ojeri, *ten.*

Cuerano, *February.*

Weer-hemska, *March.*

Heemskan, *April.*

Oneratacka, *May.*

Oneratack, *June, then men begin to sow and to plant.*

Hagarert, *July.*

Iakouvaratta, *August.*

Hatterhonagat, *September.*

Genhendasta, *October, then the grain and every thing is ripe.*

Digojenjattha, *November, then is the seed housed.*

Kitzinacka, *priest.* Also **kitsinacka**. [perhaps not Mohawk —ed.]

A MOHAWK WORD-LIST

Excerpt from A Short Account
of the Mohawk Indians

The inhabitants of this country are of two kinds: first Christians—at least so called; second, Indians. Of the Christians I shall say nothing; my design is to speak of the Indians only. These among us are again of two kinds: first the Mahakinbas, or, as they call themselves, *Kajingahaga*; second, the Mahakans, otherwise called *Agotzagena*. These two nations have different languages, which have no affinity with each other, like Dutch and Latin. These people formerly carried on a great war against each other, but since the Mahakanders were subdued by the Mahakobaas, peace has subsisted between them, and the conquered are obliged to bring a yearly contribution to the others. We live among both these kinds of Indians; and when they come to us from their country, or we go to them, they do us every act of friendship. The principal nation of all the savages and Indians hereabouts with which we have the most intercourse, is the Mahakuaas, who have laid all the other Indians near us under contribution. This nation has a very difficult language, and it costs me great pains to learn it, so as to be able to speak and preach in it fluently. There is no Christian here who understands the language thoroughly; those who have lived here long can use a kind of jargon just sufficient to carry on trade with it, but they do not understand the fundamentals of the language. I am making a vocabulary of the Mahakuaas' language, and when I am among them I ask them how things are called;

but as they are very stupid, I sometimes cannot make them understand what I want. Moreover when they tell me, one tells me the word in the infinitive mood, another in the indicative; one in the first, another in the second person; one in the present, another in the preterit. So I stand oftentimes and look, but do not know how to put it down. And as they have declensions and conjugations also, and have their augments like the Greeks, I am like one distracted, and frequently cannot tell what to do, and there is no one to set me right. I shall have to speculate in this alone, in order to become in time an Indian grammarian. When I first observed that they pronounced their words so differently, I asked the commissary of the company what it meant. He answered me that he did not know, but imagined they changed their language every two or three years; I argued against this that it could never be that a whole nation should change its language with one consent;—and, although he has been connected with them here these twenty years, he can afford me no assistance.

Aireskuoni, *the Devil.*

Anaware, *the tortoise.*

Asoronusi, asoronusi, Otskon aworouhsi reinnuha, *I thank thee, I thank thee devil, I thank thee, little uncle.*

Assirioni, *cloth-makers.*

Athzoockkuatoriaho, *a Genius, whom they esteem in the place of God.*

Charistooni, *iron-workers.*

Diatennon jawij Assirioni, hagiouisk, *Why do so many Christians do these things?*

Ihy Othkon, *I am the Devil.*

Notasten, *bags.*

Ochkari, *the bear.*

Oknaho, *the wolf.*

Otskon, *the Devil.*

Tharonhij-Jagon, *God; a Genius, whom they esteem in place of God.* Also **Tharonhijouaagon**.

Tkoschs ko aguweechon Kajingahaga kouaane Jountuckcha Othkon, *Really all the Mohawks are cunning devils.*

CLASSIFICATION OF THE IROQUOIAN LANGUAGES

NORTHERN IROQUOIAN
    Tuscarora-Nottoway
        Tuscarora
        Nottoway
    Huronian
        Huron
        Wyandot
    Laurentian
    Five Nations-Susquehannock
        Seneca
        Cayuga
        Onondaga
        Susquehannock
        Mohawk
        Oneida
SOUTHERN IROQUOIAN
    Cherokee

Sources: Lounsbury 1978, Mithun 1979, Goddard 1996.

NOTES

NOTES